Slim Goodbody's BODY BUDDIES Present...

THE AMAZING CIRCULATORY SYSTEM

How does my heart work?

CRABTREE
Publishing Company
www.crabtreebooks.com

D1544103

Crabtree Publishing Company
www.crabtreebooks.com

Series Development, Writing, and Packaging:
John Burstein Slim Goodbody Corp.

Medical Reviewer:
Christine S. Burstein, RN, MSN, FNP

Designer: Tammy West, Westgraphix

Project coordinator: Robert Walker

Editors: Mark Sachner, Water Buffalo Books
Molly Aloian

Proofreader: Adrianna Morganelli

Production coordinator: Katherine Berti

Prepress technicians: Rosie Gowsell,
Katherine Berti, Ken Wright

Picture credits:
© Getty Images: p. 27b: Karen Bleier/AFP: p. 27d
© The Granger Collection: p. 27a
© istockphoto: p. 6, 7a, 7c, 23b, 25b, 25c, 26
© Shutterstock: p. 7b, 8, 14, 16, 18–19, 20, 21b
© Slim Goodbody: cover, p. 11b, 12, 13b, 15b, 17a,
17b, 20b, 21a, 23a, 24, 27e

Ticker Character Design and Illustration:
Mike Ray, Ink Tycoon

Medical Illustrations: Colette Sands,
Render Ranch, and Mike Ray

"Slim Goodbody," "Ticker," and Render Ranch
illustrations, copyright © Slim Goodbody

Library and Archives Canada Cataloguing in Publication

Burstein, John
  The amazing circulatory system : how does my heart
work? / John Burstein.

(Slim Goodbody's body buddies)
Includes index.
ISBN 978-0-7787-4417-7 (bound).--ISBN 978-0-7787-4431-3 (pbk)

  1. Cardiovascular system--Juvenile literature.
2. Blood--Circulation--Juvenile literature. I. Title.
II. Series: Burstein, John . Slim Goodbody's body buddies.

QP103.B87 2009   j612.1   C2008-907854-3

Library of Congress Cataloging-in-Publication Data

Burstein, John.
  The amazing circulatory system : how does my heart work? /
John Burstein.
    p. cm. -- (Slim Goodbody's body buddies)
  Includes index.
  ISBN 978-0-7787-4431-3 (pbk. : alk. paper) -- ISBN 978-0-7787-4417-7
(reinforced library binding : alk. paper)
  1. Cardiovascular system--Juvenile literature. 2. Blood--Circulation--
Juvenile literature. 3. Heart--Juvenile literature. I. Title. II. Series.

  QP103.B88 2009
  612.1--dc22
                                                    2008052375

Crabtree Publishing Company

www.crabtreebooks.com   1-800-387-7650

Published in Canada
Crabtree Publishing
616 Welland Ave.
St. Catharines, Ontario
L2M 5V6

Published in the United States
Crabtree Publishing
PMB16A
350 Fifth Ave., Suite 3308
New York, NY 10118

Published in the United Kingdom
Crabtree Publishing
White Cross Mills
High Town, Lancaster
LA1 4XS

Published in Australia
Crabtree Publishing
386 Mt. Alexander Rd.
Ascot Vale (Melbourne)
VIC 3032

About the Author

John Burstein (also known as Slim Goodbody) has been entertaining and educating children
for over thirty years. His programs have been broadcast on CBS, PBS, Nickelodeon, USA,
and Discovery. He has won numerous awards including the Parent's Choice Award and the
President's Council's Fitness Leader Award. Currently, Mr. Burstein tours the country with his
multimedia live show "Bodyology." For more information, please visit **slimgoodbody.com**.

Contents

Words in **bold** are defined in the glossary on page 30.

Meet the Body Buddies

I am very happy that you are reading this book.
It means that you want to learn about your body!

I believe that the more you know about how
your body works, the prouder you will feel.

I believe that the prouder you feel, the more you
will do to take care of yourself.

I believe that the more you do to take care of
yourself, the happier and healthier you will be.

To provide you with the very best information about how your body
works, I have put together a team of good friends. I call them my
Body Buddies, and I hope they will become your Body Buddies, too!

Let me introduce them to you:

- **HUFF AND PUFF** will guide you through the lungs and the
  respiratory system.

- **TICKER** will lead you on a journey to explore the heart and
  circulatory system.

- **COGNOS** will explain how the brain and nervous system work.

- **SQUIRT** will let you in on the secrets of tiny glands that do big jobs.

- **FLEX AND STRUT** will walk you through the workings of your bones
  and muscles.

- **GURGLE** will give you a tour of the stomach and digestive system.

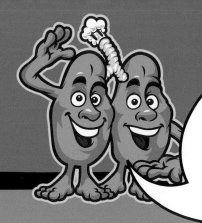

HUFF & PUFF Say...
YOUR RESPIRATORY SYSTEM IS MADE UP OF YOUR LUNGS, ALL THE AIRWAYS CONNECTED WITH THEM, AND THE MUSCLES THAT HELP YOU BREATHE.

TICKER Says...
YOUR CIRCULATORY SYSTEM IS MADE UP OF YOUR HEART, WHICH PUMPS YOUR BLOOD, AND THE TUBES, CALLED BLOOD VESSELS, THROUGH WHICH YOUR BLOOD FLOWS.

COGNOS Says...
YOUR NERVOUS SYSTEM IS MADE UP OF YOUR BRAIN, SPINAL CORD, AND ALL THE NERVES THAT RUN THROUGHOUT YOUR BODY.

SQUIRT Says...
YOUR ENDOCRINE SYSTEM IS MADE UP OF MANY DIFFERENT GLANDS THAT PRODUCE SUBSTANCES TO HELP YOUR BODY WORK RIGHT.

GURGLE Says...
YOUR DIGESTIVE SYSTEM HELPS TURN THE FOOD YOU EAT INTO ENERGY. IT INCLUDES YOUR STOMACH, LIVER, AND INTESTINES.

FLEX & STRUT Say...
YOUR MUSCULAR SYSTEM IS MADE UP OF MUSCLES THAT HELP YOUR BODY MOVE. THE SKELETAL SYSTEM IS MADE UP OF THE BONES THAT HOLD YOUR BODY UP.

LUB-DUB!

HELLO BODY BUDDIES!

LUB-DUB, LUB-DUB
LET ME INTRODUCE MYSELF.
MY NAME IS TICKER.
LUB-DUB, LUB-DUB
IF YOU HAVEN'T GUESSED IT BY NOW,
I AM A HEART.
LUB-DUB, LUB-DUB
I AM HERE TO TEACH YOU ALL ABOUT ME.
LUB-DUB, LUB-DUB
YOU WILL LEARN WHAT I DO. YOU WILL ALSO LEARN
HOW TO TAKE CARE OF ME.
LUB-DUB, LUB-DUB
THE SOUND YOU ARE HEARING IS THE MUSIC
I MAKE AS I DO MY JOB. I AM LIKE
A DRUMMER BEATING OUT
A RHYTHM ON A DRUM. I LIKE
TO CALL THIS BEAT THE
RHYTHM OF LIFE.
LUB-DUB, LUB-DUB

LUB-DUB, LUB-DUB, LUB-DUB
LUB-DUB, LUB-DUB

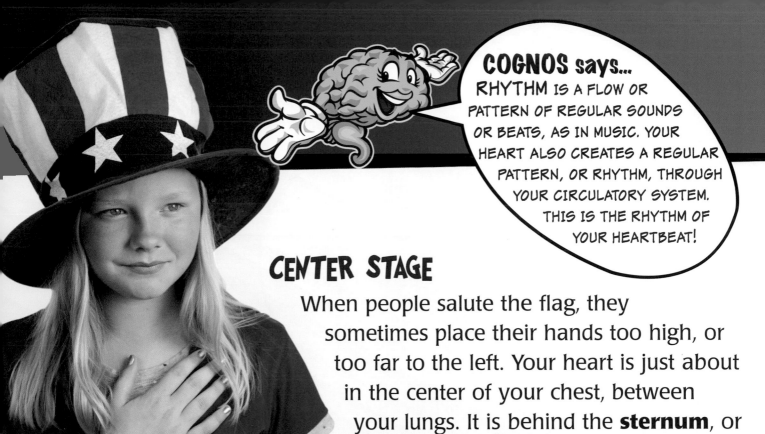

COGNOS says...
RHYTHM IS A FLOW OR PATTERN OF REGULAR SOUNDS OR BEATS, AS IN MUSIC. YOUR HEART ALSO CREATES A REGULAR PATTERN, OR RHYTHM, THROUGH YOUR CIRCULATORY SYSTEM. THIS IS THE RHYTHM OF YOUR HEARTBEAT!

CENTER STAGE

When people salute the flag, they sometimes place their hands too high, or too far to the left. Your heart is just about in the center of your chest, between your lungs. It is behind the **sternum**, or breastbone. The sternum helps protect your heart from getting hurt.

IN YOUR HAND

If you want to know how big a heart is, the answer is in your hand! Make a fist. That is about the size of your heart. Make two fists and put them together. This is how big your heart will be when you grow up.

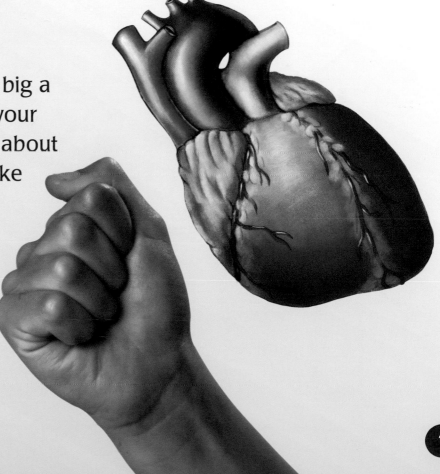

A Powerful Pumper

I AM A MIGHTY MUSCLE!

MY JOB IS TO PUMP BLOOD THROUGH THE BODY.

I WORK HARDER THAN ANY OTHER MUSCLE IN THE BODY.

LEG MUSCLES GET TO REST WHEN YOU SIT DOWN.

BACK MUSCLES GET TO REST WHEN YOU LIE DOWN.

I NEVER STOP. I NEVER SIT DOWN OR SLEEP.

IN ONE HOUR, I PUMP ABOUT 5,000 TIMES! IN A MONTH I PUMP ABOUT THREE MILLION TIMES.

I SURE AM BUSY. IT IS A GOOD THING I LOVE MY JOB!

BARRELS OF BLOOD

In a lifetime, your heart will pump about one million barrels of blood. One barrel contains about 55 gallons (208 L). Imagine 55 one-gallon bottles of milk lined up. Then multiply those 55 gallons by a million, and you might get an idea of how much blood your heart pumps in your lifetime!

MUSCLE MATTERS

Your body has three different types of muscles:

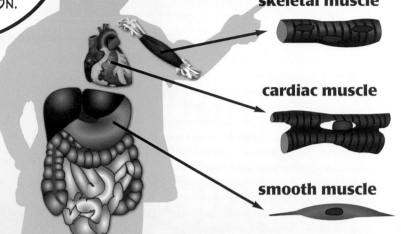

skeletal muscle

cardiac muscle

smooth muscle

1. Skeletal muscles are attached to your bones. They help you move. For example, when you chew, skeletal muscles move your jawbones.

2. The **cardiac** muscle is found only in your heart. Like smooth muscles, it works by itself. The cardiac muscle can work longer and harder than any other muscle.

3. Smooth muscles work without you telling them what to do. For example, smooth muscles push food through your small intestine.

BE A SCIENTIST

You can do a simple experiment to help you feel the three kinds of muscles working in your body.

Here is what you will need:
- Your body
- A piece of fruit

Directions:

1. Take a bite of the fruit. As you chew, place your hands on the sides of your jaw and feel your jaw muscles working. These are skeletal muscles.

2. Gently place your hand on the front of your neck, right in the middle. Swallow the chewed fruit. Your smooth muscles are pushing the food down to your stomach.

3. Slide your hand down until it covers your heart. The beating you feel is your cardiac muscle at work.

IF YOU PEEK INSIDE ME, YOU WILL SEE THAT I AM DIVIDED DOWN THE MIDDLE. I HAVE A LEFT SIDE AND A RIGHT SIDE.

EACH SIDE HAS TWO ROOMS. ONE ROOM IS ON TOP AND THE OTHER ROOM IS BELOW.

THE UPSTAIRS ROOM IS CALLED THE ATRIUM. THE DOWNSTAIRS ROOM IS CALLED THE VENTRICLE.

IN THE MIDDLE

A thick wall of muscle runs down the middle of the heart. This muscle, called the septum, separates the left and right sides of the heart.

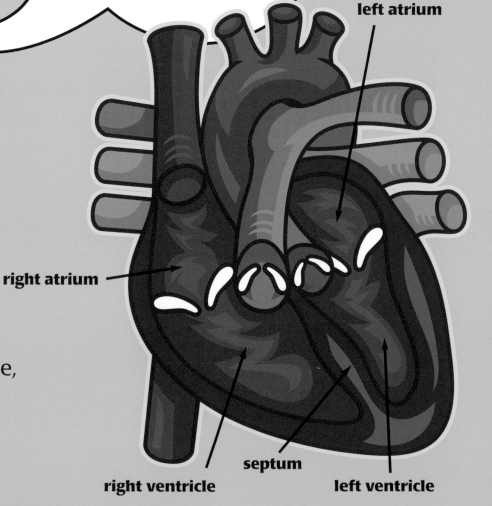

left atrium

right atrium

septum

right ventricle

left ventricle

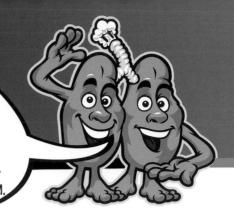

HUFF & PUFF say...
YOUR HEART IS NOT THE ONLY PART OF YOUR BODY THAT HAS A **SEPTUM** DIVIDING IT. YOUR NASAL PASSAGES ARE ALSO SEPARATED BY A WALL CALLED THE SEPTUM.

OPEN AND SHUT

The heart uses valves to help control the flow of blood. Valves are like special one-way doors. They open and let blood pass through. Then they snap shut so the blood cannot flow backward.

There are four valves in all:

1. The **tricuspid** valve.

2. The **pulmonary** valve.

3. The **aortic** valve.

4. The **mitral** valve.

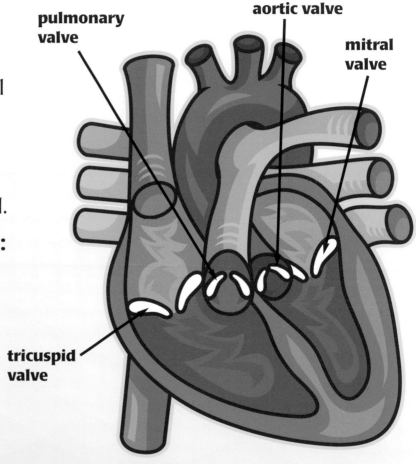

pulmonary valve

aortic valve

mitral valve

tricuspid valve

LISTEN IN

The "lub-dub" sound the heart makes comes from the valves shutting as blood flows past. The "lub" sound happens when the tricuspid and mitral valves close and blood is pumped into the ventricles. The "dub" sound happens when the aortic and pulmonary valves close after the blood has been squeezed out of the heart.

TUBES AND TUNNELS

WHEN I PUMP BLOOD OUT, IT TRAVELS THROUGH SPECIAL TUBES AND TUNNELS CALLED BLOOD VESSELS.

SOME BLOOD VESSELS, CALLED ARTERIES, CARRY BLOOD AWAY FROM ME. SOME BLOOD VESSELS, CALLED VEINS, BRING BLOOD BACK TO ME.

SOME BLOOD VESSELS CONNECT THE ARTERIES WITH THE VEINS. THESE ARE CALLED CAPILLARIES.

BLOOD VESSELS BRANCH OUT ALL THROUGH THE BODY SO BLOOD CAN REACH ALL OF YOUR CELLS.

ALL WRAPPED UP

Imagine weaving a rope out of all your arteries, veins, and capillaries. It would stretch about 60,000 miles (95,000 kilometers) – enough to circle Earth more than twice!

SQUIRT says...
CELLS ARE THE SMALLEST UNITS, OR STRUCTURES, THAT MAKE UP YOUR BODY. THEY ARE SO TINY THAT THEY CANNOT BE SEEN WITHOUT A MICROSCOPE.

OUT AND BACK

You have major arteries and veins attached to your heart. Here is what they do:

- The pulmonary artery carries blood out of your heart to your lungs.

- The aorta carries blood out of your heart to reach all the other parts of your body.

- The pulmonary veins bring blood to your heart from your lungs.

- The vena cava brings blood to your heart from all the other parts of the body.

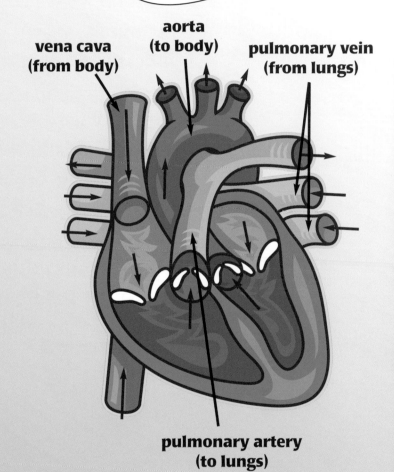

vena cava (from body)

aorta (to body)

pulmonary vein (from lungs)

pulmonary artery (to lungs)

THINNER THAN THIN

Capillaries are much thinner than your thinnest hair. You need a microscope to see them!

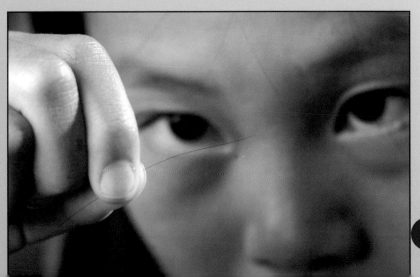

BLOOD BROTHER

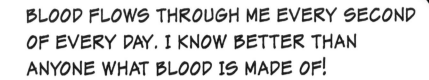

BLOOD FLOWS THROUGH ME EVERY SECOND OF EVERY DAY. I KNOW BETTER THAN ANYONE WHAT BLOOD IS MADE OF!

BLOOD IS MOSTLY MADE UP OF RED BLOOD CELLS. RED BLOOD CELLS CARRY OXYGEN.

BLOOD IS ALSO MADE UP OF WHITE BLOOD CELLS. WHITE BLOOD CELLS FIGHT GERMS TO STOP **INFECTION**.

THEN THERE ARE PLATELETS. PLATELETS ARE CELLS THAT HELP STOP BLEEDING.

FINALLY, THERE IS PLASMA. PLASMA IS A YELLOWISH LIQUID THAT CARRIES **NUTRIENTS** THROUGH THE BODY.

red blood cells

platelets

plasma

white blood cell

BONE FACTORY

Inside your bones is a jelly-like material called marrow. Marrow works like a factory. It makes blood cells. When you are young, almost all your bones have marrow that can make blood cells. When you grow up, only the marrow of certain bones, such as the spine, ribs, and pelvis, will do this work.

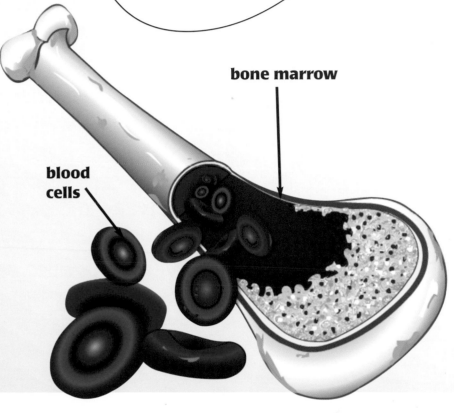

bone marrow

blood cells

BE A SCIENTIST

You can gain a better understanding of how much blood you have in your body.

Directions:

1. Fill the carton or bottle with water.

2. When the carton or bottle is full, empty the water into the pail.

3. Fill and empty the carton or bottle four more times, for a total of five times.

When you are finished, the amount of blood in the pail is about the amount of blood in your body—almost five quarts (4.7 L).

Here is what you will need:
- An empty quart- (0.9 L-) sized carton or bottle
- A pail

THE RIVER OF LIFE

THERE ARE AROUND 100 TRILLION CELLS IN THE BODY. THESE CELLS CANNOT SURVIVE WITHOUT THE HELP OF BLOOD.

EVERY CELL NEEDS FOOD TO STAY ALIVE. BLOOD DELIVERS THE MEALS THAT COME FROM THE FOOD YOU EAT.

EVERY CELL NEEDS OXYGEN TO STAY ALIVE. BLOOD DELIVERS THE OXYGEN THAT COMES INTO YOUR BODY IN THE AIR YOU BREATHE.

EVERY CELL MUST GET RID OF WASTE. BLOOD ALSO PICKS UP THE TRASH THAT IS LEFT OVER FROM THE NUTRIENTS AND OXYGEN YOUR BODY ABSORBS FROM YOUR BLOOD.

BLOOD IS LIKE A RIVER OF LIFE FLOWING UNDER YOUR SKIN!

blood cells

FEEL THE BEAT

You can feel a small beating under your skin at certain places in your body. This is called your pulse. Each beat is caused by the squeezing of your heart as it pumps out blood.

Two good places to feel your pulse are on the inside of your wrist just below the thumb and on the side of your neck. Just press in lightly.

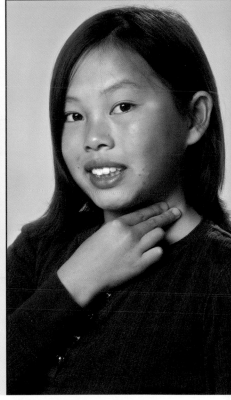

BE A SCIENTIST

You can measure your own pulse and use it to figure out what your **heart rate** is.

Here is what you will need:
- A place where you can sit quietly and relax
- A watch or a clock with a second hand

Directions:

1. Press in lightly on the inside of your wrist or the side of your neck with your **index finger** and the finger next to it.

2. Keep feeling the area under your fingers until you can detect your pulse.

3. To find out what your heart rate is, use the watch to count how many beats you feel in one minute.

THE CIRCULATORY SYSTEM

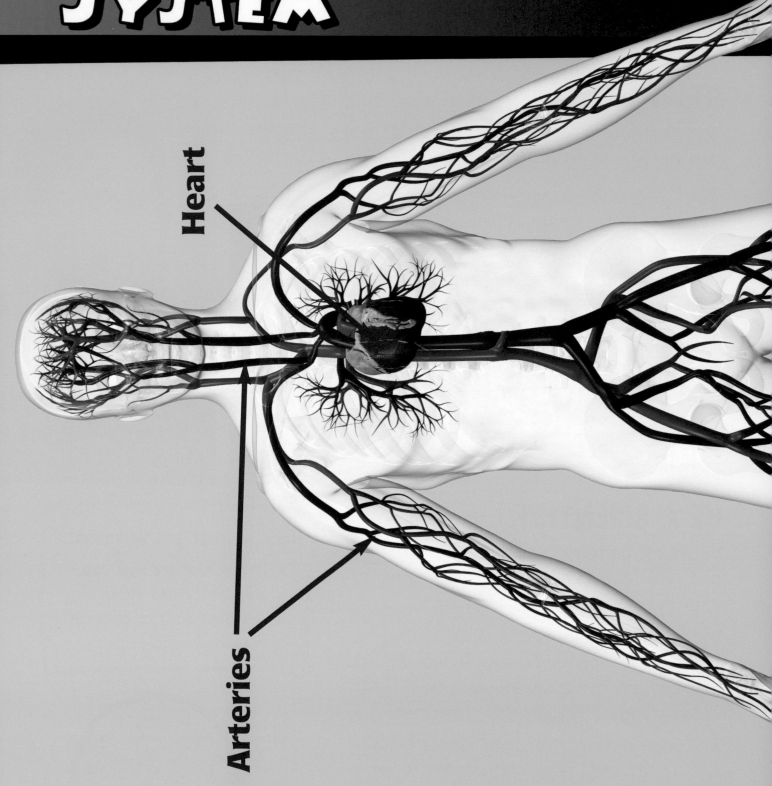

Heart

Arteries

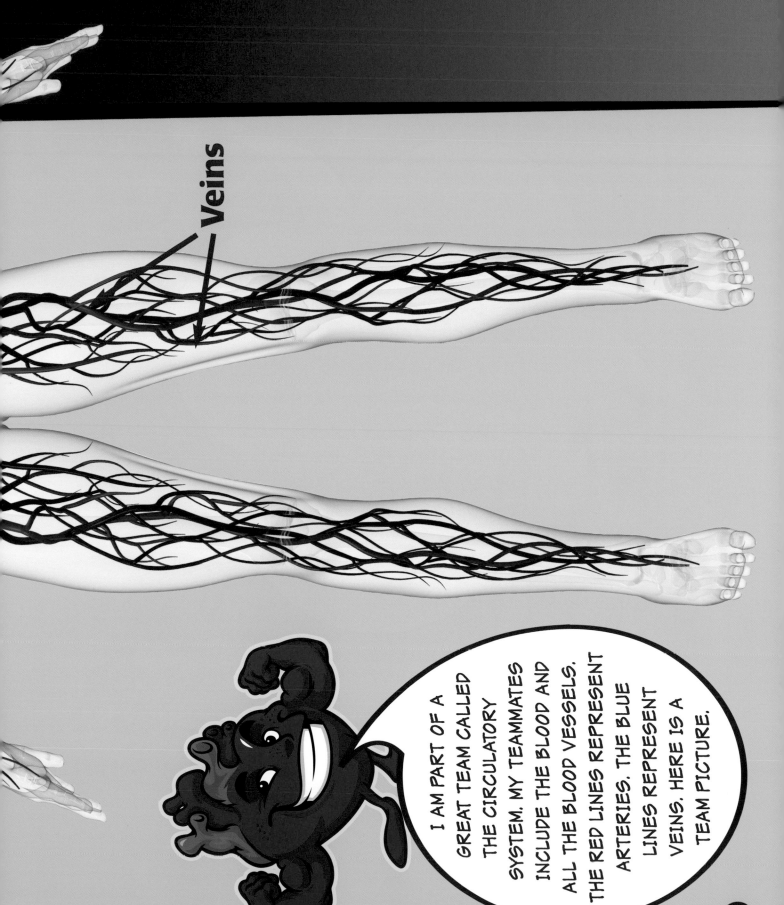

WONDERFUL WORKOUT

EXERCISE IS GOOD FOR ME.
IT MAKES ME GROW STRONGER.

WHEN I GROW STRONGER, I CAN PUMP MORE BLOOD EACH TIME I SQUEEZE.

WHEN I PUMP MORE BLOOD, MORE OXYGEN REACHES THE CELLS IN YOUR BODY.

WHEN YOUR CELLS GET MORE OXYGEN, THEY PRODUCE ENERGY MORE EASILY AND YOUR BODY STAYS HEALTHIER.

GET GOING!

To build a strong heart, do aerobic exercises for about one hour a day at least five days a week. You can play sports such as basketball, soccer, lacrosse, or hockey. You can go dancing, bike riding, swimming, skiing, or hiking. You can rake the yard, take a **brisk** walk, skateboard, or play tag.

TAKE THE TEST

When you do these exercises, you want your heart to work hard, but not too hard. If you cannot talk easily because you are too out of breath, you are working too hard.

GETTING A BOOST

When you exercise, your body makes more red blood cells to help carry more oxygen. Your body also grows more capillaries to help deliver the oxygen faster.

ENERGY FOR ME

I NEED ENERGY TO DO MY WORK. ENERGY COMES FROM FOOD.

FOODS SUCH AS FRUITS, VEGETABLES, AND WHOLE GRAINS ARE GOOD FOR ME.

THEY ARE PACKED WITH POWER.

FOODS SUCH AS LEAN MEAT, CHICKEN, FISH, BEANS, AND LOW-FAT MILK ALSO KEEP ME HEALTHY.

WHAT IS CHOLESTEROL?

Cholesterol is a type of fat. It is carried through your body by your blood. Some cholesterol is made by your liver. Some comes from foods you eat. The right amount and right kind of cholesterol helps your brain, skin, and other organs grow and do their jobs.

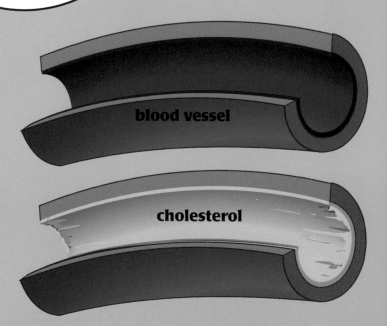

blood vessel

cholesterol

SLOW FLOW

If you have too much of the wrong kind of cholesterol in your blood, it may stick to the walls of your blood vessels. This can make your blood vessels narrower and slow the flow of blood to important body parts such as your heart and brain. When this happens over many years, these parts may become damaged.

IN CONTROL OF CHOLESTEROL

Here are some eating tips to help you control the cholesterol in your body.

Eat more:

Try to eat a lot of fruits, vegetables, and grains. They do not have any cholesterol.

Avoid:

Try to avoid too many fatty foods such as fried chicken, French fries, or bacon. Stay away from too much butter, margarine, or cream. Also avoid drinking a lot of whole milk and shakes.

CUT THE CAFFEINE

Caffeine is a chemical in coffee and many sodas. Too much caffeine is not good for your heart. It can make your heart pump faster than normal. It can make you feel nervous. It can also make it hard to fall asleep. The best drinks are water and low-fat milk, which do not contain caffeine.

SODA

UH-OH!

HEARTS ARE STRONG, BUT SOMETIMES THEY GET SICK.

SOMETIMES THE HEART MUSCLE GETS WEAK. SOMETIMES THE HEART STARTS BEATING TOO SLOW OR TOO FAST. WHEN HEARTS GET SICK, DOCTORS WORK HARD TO MAKE THEM BETTER.

SOMETIMES HEARTS NEED SPECIAL MEDICINE. SOMETIMES HEARTS MUST BE OPERATED ON. SOMETIMES HEARTS GET BETTER WITH BETTER FOODS AND EXERCISES.

DOCTORS DO SPECIAL TESTS TO FIND OUT WHAT IS WRONG AND WHAT CAN HELP.

WITH THE RIGHT FOOD, MEDICINE, AND EXERCISE, MOST SICK HEARTS GET BETTER!

TICKER says...

YOUR BLOOD PRESSURE IS THE PRESSURE, OR FORCE, OF YOUR BLOOD AGAINST THE WALLS OF OUR BLOOD VESSELS. TOO MUCH OR TOO LITTLE PRESSURE CAN MEAN THAT YOUR HEART IS WORKING EITHER TOO HARD OR NOT HARD ENOUGH TO PUMP BLOOD TO ALL THE PARTS OF YOUR BODY.

ATTACK

Your heart pumps blood to your body. It also pumps blood to itself. Like your body's other cells, cells that make up your heart need oxygen. A heart attack can happen when a major blood vessel gets blocked and cuts off the blood flow to a part of the heart. If the blood flow is not fixed very soon, that part of the heart muscle loses oxygen, becomes damaged, and begins to die. If the problem is fixed right away, the heart can get well again.

cholesterol

blocked blood vessel

CHECKING IN

When you have a checkup, your doctor or nurse checks on the health of your heart. She listens to it with a **stethoscope** to be sure the beat is steady and strong. She also uses a special medical tool called a blood pressure cuff to check the force of the blood pushing against the walls of the arteries in your arm. This is called taking your blood pressure. Taking your blood pressure helps the doctor know just how hard your heart is working to get its job done.

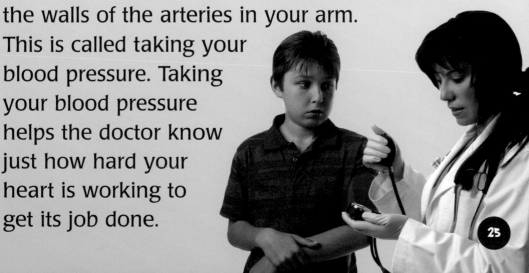

A Little Heart History

SCIENTISTS HAVE STUDIED ME FOR A LONG TIME.

FOR MANY YEARS, NOBODY UNDERSTOOD HOW I WORKED.

TODAY PEOPLE KNOW MUCH MORE ABOUT ME. IT IS EXCITING TO IMAGINE HOW MUCH MORE THEY WILL LEARN IN THE FUTURE.

ANCIENT BELIEFS

In ancient Egypt, people believed I took care of thinking and controlled feelings or emotions. They did not know that these were handled by the brain!

In ancient China, people thought I was the center for happiness.

The ancient Greeks thought my job was to heat up the blood and burn away any parts of it that were not pure.

In the **Middle Ages**, people believed the liver had to keep making new blood. They did not know about circulation.

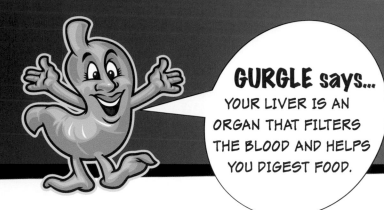

GURGLE says...
YOUR LIVER IS AN ORGAN THAT FILTERS THE BLOOD AND HELPS YOU DIGEST FOOD.

HEART HEROES

Dr. William Harvey was the first scientist to figure out how blood circulated through the body. His discovery took place in 1628, almost 400 years ago.

The first successful heart operation took place in 1896, when Dr. Ludwig Rehn stitched up a wound in the heart of a young German soldier.

In 1964, Dr. Christiaan Barnard took the heart of a 25-year-old woman who had died after an auto accident and placed it into the chest of a 55-year-old man dying of heart damage. This was the first successful heart transplant operation.

In 1982, the first permanent artificial heart was placed inside a 61-year-old dentist. The heart was designed by Dr. Robert Jarvik and called the Jarvik-7.

FABULOUS PHRASES

BEFORE YOU GO, I WANT TO PLAY A GAME.

IN THE BOX BELOW YOU WILL SEE EIGHT PHRASES.

EACH PHRASE HAS THE WORD "HEART" IN IT.

WE WILL START A SENTENCE AND YOU TRY
TO FILL IN THE BLANK USING ONE OF THE PHRASES.

FOR EXAMPLE, IF THE SENTENCE NUMBER I IS:
ACTORS IN A PLAY LEARN ALL THEIR LINES _____ .

YOU WOULD CHOOSE THE PHRASE "A": "BY HEART." GOT IT?

7. Actors in a play learn all their lines _____.

2. If someone you love hurts your feelings you might have a _____.

3. If someone is very nice, people might say she has a _____.

4. If you change your feelings about something, people might say you had a _____.

5. When you believe something deeply, you believe it from the _____.

6. When you promise to do something, you might _____.

7. A cute puppy can _____.

8. If you are talking honestly with someone, you are having a _____.

A. By heart	**D.** Heart-to-heart	**G.** Cross your heart
B. Change of heart	**E.** Melt your heart	**H.** Bottom of your
C. Broken heart	**F.** Heart of gold	heart

ANSWERS: 1A, 2C, 3F, 4B, 5H, 6G, 7E, 8D

Amazing Facts About Your Heart

THE AORTA IS THE LARGEST ARTERY IN THE BODY. THE AORTA HAS ABOUT THE SAME DIAMETER, OR DISTANCE ACROSS, AS A GARDEN HOSE.

A DOCTOR WHO TAKES CARE OF THE HEART (CARDIAC MUSCLE) IS CALLED A CARDIOLOGIST.

YOUR HEART IS STRONG ENOUGH TO PUMP A JET OF BLOOD ALMOST 6 FEET (2 METERS) UP IN THE AIR.

EXERCISE ACTUALLY INCREASES THE SIZE OF YOUR HEART.

THE CROCODILE WAS THE FIRST ANIMAL TO DEVELOP A FOUR-CHAMBERED HEART LIKE OURS.

BLOOD CIRCULATES THROUGH YOUR BODY THOUSANDS OF TIMES A DAY.

MOST HEART ATTACKS OCCUR BETWEEN THE HOURS OF 8:00 AND 9:00 A.M.

BY THE TIME YOU ARE 70 YEARS OLD, YOUR HEART WILL BEAT MORE THAN 2.5 BILLION TIMES.

A GOOD, DEEP LAUGH ATTACK CAN HELP BLOOD VESSEL WALLS RELAX. WHEN BLOOD VESSELS ARE RELAXED, THEY ALLOW BLOOD TO FLOW MORE EASILY.

YOUR BLOOD PRESSURE CHANGES DURING THE DAY. IT IS LOWEST AS YOU SLEEP AND RISES WHEN YOU GET UP AND YOUR HEART BEGINS TO WORK HARDER.

BLOOD PRESSURE CAN RISE WHEN YOU ARE EXCITED, NERVOUS, OR ACTIVE.

GLOSSARY

aortic Having to do with the aorta, which is the largest blood vessel in the human body. The aortic valve controls the flow of blood into the aorta

brisk Lively or fast

cardiac Anything having to do with the heart

heart rate The number of times the heart beats in a certain amount of time, usually a minute

index finger The finger that is next to the thumb

infection The attack on healthy parts of your body by germs. Infections can lead to injury or disease and should be cleaned and treated with medicine

Middle Ages The period of European history usually thought of as falling between about the year 500 and 1400–1500 A.D.

mitral Having to do with the shape of a bishop's hat, or miter, which has a triangular shape. The mitral valve contains flaps that have a triangular shape

nutrients Sources of nourishment and energy, especially from the food we eat

pulmonary Anything having to do with the lungs or breathing. The pulmonary valve controls the flow of blood that will go to the lungs

sternum A long, flat bone in the center of the chest that supports most of the ribs and protects the heart and lungs

stethoscope An instrument used to listen to sounds produced inside your body, usually by your heart and lungs

tricuspid Having to do with three. The tricuspid valve has three flaps that control the flow of blood in the heart

FOR MORE INFORMATION

BOOKS

Active Kids (Kid Power). Kathryn Smithyman (author), Bobbie Kalman (author), Marc Crabtree (illustrator). Crabtree Publishing.

Dr. Frankenstein's Human Body Book. Richard Walker. DK Publishing.

The Heart: Our Circulatory System. Seymour Simon. Collins.

The Incredible Human Body. Esther Weiner. Scholastic Inc.

The Usborne Complete Book of the Human Body. Anna Claybourne (author), Stephen Moncrieff (illustrator), Juliet Percival (illustrator). Usborne Books.

What Happens When Your Heart Beats? (How Your Body Works). Jacqui Bailey. PowerKids Press.

WEBSITES

American Heart Association
www.americanheart.org/presenter.jhtml?identifier=3028650
This website has many activities and downloadable worksheets to help you keep your heart healthy.

Kids Health for Kids
kidshealth.org/kid/htbw/heart.html
Check out this website for information on your heart and circulatory system.

Minneapolis Heart Foundation
www.mplsheartfoundation.org/kids/
Visit this website for some interactive learning about your heart and a free healthy heart certificate.

Slim Goodbody
www.slimgoodbody.com
Discover loads of fun and free downloads for kids, teachers, and parents.

INDEX

Printed in the U.S.A. - CG